Messiah's Last Call

Table of Contents

Dr. John Neuhaus III

Messiah's Last Call

ISBN 979-8-89034-421-2 (paperback)
ISBN 979-8-89034-423-6 (digital)

Messiah's Last Call

*You also must be ready, because the Son of man will come
at an hour when you do not expect him.*
Luke 12:40

Dr. John Neuhaus III

Acknowledgements

I would like to express my sincere gratitude and love for my wife—my greatest supporter in this life—Apostle Dr. Kim A. Neuhaus for her inspiration, encouragement, and prophetic revelation; to my daughter, Apostle Shelly Stephenson, for her loyalty and excellence, and for editing this book; and to Bryan and Yulonda Galloway Mansaray for their loyalty, faithfulness, and support for this book and the cause of Christ.

Dr. John Neuhaus III

Foreword

In the concentrated understanding of the revelation of the kingdom, God revealed His vision to us. Standing in the throne of God and His glory, completely surrounded and saturated by Him, we were covered by God completely, and totally surrounded in His glory. In His glory we were prepared and perfected as was Abram and as was Sarai, in the magnificence and the maturation of this great calling for the building of the kingdom of God.

Along with the majestic ministry of the gospel of the kingdom, God has also called us to cover His people, to be the Father and Mother of leaders in ministry and in business. We shepherd shepherds. We train, ordain, appoint, and send His chosen vessels throughout the world with righteousness, authenticity, and integrity to order and establish His eternal kingdom government forever (Is. 4; Is. 9; Is 54; Is. 60; Is. 61; Eph. 2; Eph. 4; Rev. 1).

The birthing of *Messiah's Last Call* is a Word from the throne of God and is a work of true apostolic and prophetic mastery. It is in this authority and by the calling and appointment of and by Jesus Himself, that the foundational principles of the message of the kingdom is revealed by Apostle Dr. John Neuhaus. This message resounds profoundly in *Messiah's Last Call*.

I am tremendously thankful for and honored by the wisdom that Apostle Dr. John Neuhaus has been given by God to speak to the subject matter of God's appointed vessels in *Messiah's Last Call*. He is a man of God who has never wavered from what God has revealed to him. He has the word of God in His heart and in His mouth. The revelation of the kingdom and the knowledge of the Word of God in him is unmatched. He knows the order of God and the kingdom of God; he knows the order of heaven; he knows the order of Melchizedek; he knows God and God knows him. God speaks to him daily.

Messiah's Last Call is God's holy Word of righteousness. This message is timely. It is relevant. The body of Christ must have God's truth, authenticity, and accuracy in its preparation for the kingdom. As the body of Christ, you will be inspired and empowered by the present kingdom truths of *Messiah's Last Call*.

My husband, Apostle Dr. John Neuhaus, for over forty years has been inspired by God. He is a profound servant of the most high God and is God's Father to the nations.

Apostle & Prophet Dr. Kim A. Neuhaus

Table of Contents

Introduction

From the generation of Adam until now, mankind has arrived at the last and final generation which will bring forth the return of the long-awaited Messiah, Jesus Christ. He will then sit upon the throne of His father David judging in truth and hastening righteousness. The reign of Christ, with His loyal and faithful saints of all ages, will bring forth the end of human government and the beginning of divine government. Countless things that Jesus and the prophets have spoken of will be fulfilled in this generation. The time we are now living in is the most unique generation, concerning the Church, that has ever existed. We have before us six thousand years of biblical history, including all the journeys and written movements of the people of God. No generation before us has been born into the revelation, the technology, and the witness that this generation has received.

In this hour there are many spiritual entities and movements to choose from. However, we must remember that old things tend to decay and lose the primary vision of what they once were, having only a form or appearance of godliness but denying its power (2 Tim. 3:5). Many have become like the nation of Israel in Jesus's time, trees with leaves but no fruit (Matt. 21:19). When spiritual movements can no longer produce the desired fruit that the Father intends, He will command that that tree or nation be cut down and then the Father will often do a new thing that will come suddenly and quickly. We are encouraged to earnestly seek the Lord to know if we are following the right or righteous thing, or leadership, chosen for us by God. When the Father does a new thing in the earth, we have no natural sign like the children of Israel had—no cloud or pillar of fire to follow. As a mature kingdom people, it is our responsibility to discern the new thing the Father does in the earth through our spirit and diligent seeking. "Behold, I will do a new thing, Now it shall spring forth; Shall you not know it" (Isa. 43:19 NKJV)?

This writing is set forth to give definition and clarity to what we follow, who we follow, and how we follow. Jesus warns us often not to be deceived by false prophets and false teachers, "For many will come saying, 'I am the Christ' or 'I am anointed of the Lord,'" (Luke 20:35) but, in truth, are deceivers or ignorant of the truth. We need the anointing, but this is not the criteria we should follow; the criteria we will explain later. We must know and be assured that who or what we follow is vital to our final deliverance as a people who are accounted worthy to obtain the resurrection of the living and the dead in Christ, prepared to enter the next age. In our present day, many have built false and deceptive religious systems, some knowingly and some unknowingly, unaware that they are building and laboring in vain. Religious systems are often trendy, appealing, and look good outwardly; yet, like what King David had to realize, they are not following the due and necessary order that God requires.

The seed of the Word of God has been published, sown, and planted in all the earth among the nations. Now, God's people must prepare to transition into a new day which will fulfill the last and final journey as the people of God gather together, as one, to keep the last and final feast, the Feast of Tabernacles or the Feast of Harvest. This is more than a harvest of new souls, as most believers adhere to, it is also a gathering together in Christ of the elect, the literal seed of Abraham, that have become a company of nations and a multitude of people in the midst of the earth (Gen. 48:16).

God promised Abraham that He would multiply and bless his offspring and redeem them by bringing the promised seed into the New Covenant. He swore He would fulfill what He promised to the house of Israel; to gather the outcasts and the lost sheep of the house of Israel, the ten lost tribes that God divorced and cut off from being sons and daughters because they broke his covenant. They became a wild olive tree scattered throughout the nations and cut off from the stock of Israel, yet God promised that He would gather those that had been cast out and scattered among the nations and graft them back into their own olive tree. He will bring them into covenant once again where all that believe will receive the spirit of adoption through the new covenant and will once again be called the sons of the living God (Hos. 1:9-11; Rom. 9:4). God furthered this promise to Jacob in his dream of angels. "And he dreamed, and behold a ladder set up on the earth, and the top of it reached to heaven: and behold the angels of God ascending and descending on it. And, behold, the Lord stood above it, and said, I am the Lord God of Abraham thy father, and the God of Isaac: the land whereon thou liest, to thee will I give it, and to thy seed; And thy seed shall be as the dust of the earth, and thou shalt spread abroad to the west, and to the east, and to the north, and to the south: and in thee and in thy seed shall all the families of the earth be blessed" (Gen. 28:12-14 KJV).

In the end of days, the Father will sift among the nations and gather the lost sheep of the house of Israel that Jesus spoke about in Matthew 15:24 and the twelve tribes which were scattered abroad that the Apostle James also spoke about in James 1:1. This will be a gathering together of the seed of Abraham, the father of many nations, including the promised multitudes of sons and daughters that have been scattered throughout the earth over millennia, those called even in our time the Diaspora or dispersion. "For thus saith the Lord GOD; Behold, I, *even* I, will both search my sheep, and seek them out. As a shepherd seeketh out his flock in the day that he is among his sheep *that are* scattered; so will I seek out my sheep, and will deliver them out of all places where they have been scattered in the cloudy and dark day. And I will bring them out from the people, and gather them from the countries, and will bring them to their own land, and feed them upon the mountains of Israel by the rivers, and in all the inhabited places of the country" (Ezek. 34:11-13 KJV). We now live "in the cloudy and dark day" where darkness has covered the earth and obscured many truths of the gospel, but God's promise to Abraham, that He would gather his seed and bring them into covenant, will be fulfilled in this great last day harvest of the promised seed.

Most all those in Christ are the promised and literal seed of Abraham. The Galatians were a gentile church in a region filled with the outcasts of Israel and the lost sheep of Israel, but the Apostle Paul wrote this in his letter to them, "Now we, brethren, as Isaac was, are the children of promise" (Gal. 4:28 KJV). This will be an end-time harvest of fully mature sons and daughters, the elect, grown up into His fullness; a royal priesthood company in His image that will enter the kingdom age prepared to rule and reign with the Lord Jesus in their midst.

Comprehending the King and His Kingdom

Everything written in this book centers on a revelation of the kingdom of God, when it will appear, how it will operate in the earth, who the leaders will be that will help us cross over from the age of grace to the age of the kingdom, and who will be found worthy to enter this final age that is nearer than many suppose or imagine.

The Father is calling every believer to align themselves and prepare for the coming of Christ's earthly kingdom, which will spread from sea to sea and to the ends of the earth (Ps. 72:8).

The Church Formed at Pentecost Was a Way God's People Had Never Been Before

On the day of Pentecost, the Father formed the new church that began to operate in a completely new way. Jesus had laid the foundation of his house with a functioning body of believers, which operated under the newly formed leadership.

In that same season the Father then raised up his chosen vessel the apostle Paul, revealing a completely new revelation and teaching that we call the grace of God. This revelation laid a new foundation that brought salvation and deliverance to this new body of believers. The people that followed this new order and government were first called Christians in Antioch meaning children of the way. The apostles began to instruct all of the churches in the new teaching, concerning the forgiveness of sins and the grace of God that is received by faith (as there were those who believed salvation was by works of righteousness or good deeds). This new teaching of grace came with much persecution and opposition from the old religious order, which was eradicated when Jesus offered himself up for the sins of the world. The grace of God was not given that men would have an excuse for their sins without truly repenting of their sins, the doctrine and teaching of grace was given that God's people would be convicted of their sins by the Holy Spirit and see their sins, confess their sins, repent and be forgiven and fully cleansed, having their sins forever washed away by the blood of Jesus.

Grace was given that the Lord's people would live and walk in the truth and so might learn to live a life free from the condemnation of a sin-filled life. In other words, the teaching of grace was given for the Lord to separate to himself a holy people, prepared for kingdom living with the ability and understanding to teach the nations and the sinners of the world the righteous ways of the Lord.

The Father Gave us Grace To Prepare Us To Be A Kingdom People

For the grace of God that brings salvation has appeared to all men, teaching us that, denying ungodliness and worldly lusts, we should live soberly, righteously, and godly in the present age, looking for the blessed hope and glorious appearing of our great God and Savior Jesus Christ, who gave Himself for us, that He might redeem us (liberate us) from every lawless deed and purify for Himself *His* own special people, zealous for good works (Titus 2:11-15 NKJV).

It has taken two thousand years of revelation and impartation through the grace of God for the Father to form and bring forth a fully mature generation of saints which the apostle Peter called a chosen generation, a royal priesthood, a holy nation, a people belonging to God.

But you are a chosen generation, a royal priesthood, a holy nation, a people belonging to God, that you may declare the praises of him who called you out of darkness into his wonderful light (1 Peter 2:9-10 NIV).

Let Us Prepare to Receive An Abundant Entrance Into Christ's Kingdom

Wherefore the rather, brethren, give diligence to make your calling and election sure: for if ye do these things, ye shall never fall: For so an entrance shall be ministered unto you abundantly into the everlasting kingdom of our Lord and Savior Jesus Christ. Wherefore I will not be negligent to put you always in remembrance of these things, though ye know them, and be established in the present truth (2 Peter 1:10-13).

There is a present truth that God has reserved for this generation that no other generation has received so it is vital that we seek the Lord for the truth he has purposed for our generation.

There will be no peace on the earth until the Lord Jesus returns to strike through all evil kings in the day of his wrath and sits on the throne of David administering justice and judgment throughout the earth as the governor of all nations.

Jesus Is Coming To Judge The World In Righteousness

> O worship the Lord in the beauty of holiness: fear before him, all the earth. Say among the heathen that the Lord reigns: the world also shall be established that it shall not be moved: he shall judge the people righteously. Let the heavens rejoice, and let the earth be glad; let the sea roar, and the fulness thereof. Let the field be joyful, and all that is therein: then shall all the trees of the wood rejoice Before the Lord: for he cometh, for he cometh to judge the earth: he shall judge the world with righteousness, and the people with his truth (Ps. 96:9, 97:1).

The Last Generation When Jesus Returns

Jesus said that the last generation before his return would live in very evil times. Jesus likened it to the days of Noah when the whole earth was filled with violence, and all flesh had corrupted the Lord's way upon the earth. The world was so corrupt that they no longer feared the judgment of the Lord for the consequences of their evil and corrupt ways. Those that bore children lost the ability to teach their children the righteous ways of God, which caused God to end and destroy the world by bringing in a flood upon the ungodly (Gen. 6:5-13; 2 Peter 2:5).

The prophet Joel told us that as the day of the Lord's return draws near there will be multitudes and multitudes of people in the valley of decision (Joel 3:14). In the end of days, the world would become to untold millions like a great valley, an extremely low and depressed place. As God arises to shake terribly the earth the Lord in his wisdom and mercy will use this time of shaking and upheaval to bring all peoples and nations to a place of decision that they might turn to God in faith and repentance with all of their hearts and find mercy in the day of trouble, for in that time during that great shaking whosever will call on the name of the Lord shall be delivered. As the Father shakes the heavens (spiritual things) and the earth (natural things), the sea and dry land (peoples and nations) that in that time "The LORD will be the hope of his people and the strength of the children of Israel" and they will know that the Lord is dwelling in Zion (Joel 3:16).

Who Will Enter The Kingdom of Heaven?

This day we live in is a day of separation. This is a time when the Lord is thoroughly cleansing His house to separate the wheat from the chaff (which was once a part of the wheat). The Lord is examining His house to separate the holy from the unholy, and the righteous from the unrighteous. The chaff represents religious people, who have a form of godliness, but possess no power to produce the fruits of righteousness or the truth they profess with their mouths (2 Tim. 3). Though they claim to know the Lord, their hearts are far from him (Matt.

15:8). We live in an hour when the Lord is coming to judge all people with the truths of his word (John 12:48). In the day of the Lord's coming, all things that have been done in darkness will be brought to the light. It will be revealed that those that only profess Christ and do not have the fruits of righteousness and truth abiding in them, will be unprepared to meet a holy God or live in his kingdom.

The rains and storms of lawlessness and rebellion against the ways of God are quickly spreading throughout the earth.

In this day of tribulation and storms there are two kinds of people Jesus recognizes, those he calls wise and those he calls foolish; the storms are coming to both the wise and the foolish. Those that have heard the gospel and the teachings of the Lord Jesus will build their house on a true revelation of Christ. Those that will be wise in this life will hear Christ's sayings and perform them in their lives, believing and obeying the gospel and his words with all of their hearts. In so doing, they will receive a true revelation of Jesus the rock and foundation of their faith. The wise are those that will have taken the effort to dig deep in the word of God, making sure they have built their houses on a solid foundation and a true revelation of Christ their savior. Those that are foolish are those that hear the Lord's words and choose to disobey him.

"But why do you call Me 'Lord, Lord,' and not do the things which I say? Whoever comes to Me, and hears My sayings and does them, I will show you whom he is like: He is like a man building a house, who dug deep and laid the foundation on the rock. And when the flood arose, the stream beat vehemently against that house, and could not shake it, for it was founded on the rock. But he who heard and did nothing is like a man who built a house on the earth without a foundation, against which the stream beat vehemently; and immediately it fell. And the ruin of that house was great (Luke 6:46-49 NKJV).

12

Scripture References
Chapter One

Ps 72:8 Dominion From Sea to Sea

Titus 2:11-15 NKJV Grace Brings Us to Salvation

1 Peter 2:9-10 NIV A Chosen Generation

2 Peter 1:10-13 Make Your Calling and Election Sure

Ps. 96:9 Tremble Before Him

Ps. 97:1 The Lord Reigns

Gen. 6:5-13 The Wickedness of Man Was Great

2 Peter 2:5 They Have Gone Astray

Joel 3:14 The Valley of Decision

Joel 3:16 The Hope of His People

2 Tim. 3 Godlessness in the Last Days

Matt. 15:8 Hearts are Far From Him

John 12:48 The Word Will Judge

Luke 6:4649 The House on the Rock

Pre-Qualified Vessels

From the time of Christ's birth and ascension, the Church began its Pentecostal season and outpouring of the Holy Spirit upon all flesh. From the day of Pentecost until now, the intent of the Father, for the last two thousand years, was to visit the nations in a season of visitations, revivals, and sovereign moves of the Holy Spirit throughout the earth. God, the Father, sent Jesus, His only true son, to proclaim His Father's kingdom and to send the Holy Spirit to His people, which began the season of visitation. The intent, according to the apostle Peter, was to bring out from among the nations a people for His name adorned with His nature (Acts 15:14). It was through these visitations and heaven-sent rains that the Father planted the seeds of the coming kingdom into the hearts of peoples from all nations. The Lord's command to His chosen apostles was to preach and publish the gospel among all nations, which has now been accomplished. This fulfills the forty Jubilees of a two-thousand-year wilderness and testing season of the Church's wanderings and the completion of the Feast of Pentecost.

Prophet Hosea gives us great prophetic insight concerning the times and seasons of the Lord for the end-time church, a time when we will see a great return to the Lord, "Come, and let us return unto the Lord: for he has torn, and he will heal us; he hath smitten, and he will bind us up. After two days will he revive us: in the third day he will raise us up, and we shall live in his sight. Then shall we know if we follow on to know the Lord" (Hos. 6:1-3 KJV). For a span of two thousand years (or two prophetic days) the prophet tells us that God would allow His people to be torn and smitten; which is historically true, and yet with a promise that in the end the Lord will come and heal us and bind us together as a bundle of wheat, gathering us into His barn, which is a place of safety, preservation, and reproduction. It will be a time when the saints of all ages will enter into the third day. In that soon-coming day, the last trumpet will sound, the resurrection of the just will take place, and His people will dwell together with Him as one. At that time, the saints and overcomers of all ages will enter the kingdom and live in His sight as a holy nation and redeemed people. The prophet tells us that we will know and discern the times if we follow on to know the Lord and, by doing so, are able to recognize the times as a people ready and prepared for His coming.

In this day, as in Jesus's day, many false prophets have gone out into the world with the same agenda that God's prophets, such as Ezekiel and Jeremiah, rebuked. They asserted that the walls and religious systems of their day that the false prophets were building were covered with whitewash to make them look appealing outwardly and yet they were leading the people astray. The false prophets made it appear that what they were supposedly building for the Lord would protect the people from war, coming storms, and winds of persecution. The true prophets had a word for those false teachers and false prophets that seduced the people by telling them that the Lord had spoken when the Lord had not spoken and by building their church programs with falsehoods and false promises which had no strength to sustain. They were using untempered mortar building religious systems that would not hold together in the day of judgment and calamity. "It is definitely because they have misled My people by saying, 'Peace!' when there is no peace (no safety or true protection). And when anyone builds a wall, behold, they plaster it over with whitewash; *so,* tell those who plaster *it* over with whitewash, that it will fall. A flooding rain will come, and you, O hailstones, will fall; and a violent wind will break out. Behold, when the wall has fallen, will you not be asked, "Where is the plaster with which you plastered *it*" (Ezek.13:10-13 NAS)? In other words, when their false promises fail, the people will then ask the builders, "Where is the system you told us we could trust in? Where is the system you said would protect us?"

The leaders of the religious system of Jesus's day, though they were experts in the Law (the Word of God), did not recognize their High Priest and rightful King when He appeared the first time; and should we not think that this could take place once again and that some, or many, will be surprised when they end up as the foolish virgins in Matthew 25 who were refused entrance and rejected from the kingdom age? We must be assured in this hour that the Father has prepared, chosen, and pre-qualified vessels that have a revelation and know the way the people of God should go and move forward. We must be diligent to make our calling and election sure and steadfast and have a willingness to be instructed and led a way that we have never been before.

Scripture References
Chapter Two

Acts 15:14 Brought Out From the Nations
Hos. 6:1-3 KJV Insight For the End-Time Church
Ezek.13:10-13 NAS Religious Systems That Cannot Stand

A Seed Will Serve Him

In the Holy Scriptures there are countless futuristic prophecies that the prophets of old have spoken and recorded for future generations, many of which have come to pass and many that will be fulfilled in the last generation just prior to the Lord's returns. The Apostle Peter prophesied a salvation and divine deliverance ready to be revealed and disclosed in the last time (1 Pet. 1:5). The revealing or revelation of this writing is not a widely known or circulated teaching because it is a prophetic word shut up and sealed until the end only to be fulfilled and revealed in the last generation. It is a heavenly cry and voice to those that have an ear to hear what the Spirit is saying to the churches. It is a call to the nations for God's people to prepare and be ready to see the Lord's face. David prophesied of a time when the kingdom would be the Lord's and that He would be governor among the nations declaring also that a seed would serve Him which would be accounted to the Lord for a generation or a numbered and chosen generation (Ps. 22:28, 31).

Jesus likened the kingdom to a very tiny seed, less than all the seeds, but when it was sown, it grew greater than all the seeds sending out great branches. We know the seed is the Word of God that was planted into the lives of twelve men that at the time looked small and insignificant compared to the great call and challenge that was ahead, yet that seed took root in the hearts of men, grew, and multiplied. Now, in this final generation, the seed of God's Word has grown up and matured in the hearts of men purposed to bring forth a worthy company of qualified kingdom sons and daughters called to gather in the harvest of the last hour (Matt. 20:2-16).

From its inception, the Church has, for the most part, taught that Heaven is our final destination with little teaching about the saints' true inheritance, plainly revealed by the Lord Himself, that the meek will inherit the earth. The saints' inheritance is the kingdom of God and by our entrance into the kingdom of God, we receive all the promises given to Abraham and his seed (Matt. 25:34). Even in the natural world, when one is appointed, it is usually because they have endured a time of training and testing by a master and in order to receive a promotion, they must first prove they are qualified for the position they have trained for. In some cases, they may be examined by other already trained ones delegated by the master to see if they are prepared to take up a position of rule and authority. Official appointments are given to those that have been found faithful. Jesus taught and demonstrated in His earthly life the principle of loyalty and faithfulness saying, "He that is faithful over a little will be made ruler over much" (Matt. 25:23).

The writer to the Hebrews tells us that we need to consider and attentively observe our Apostle and High Priest, that we confess as our Savior, who has been sent to us from Heaven appointed as the heir of all things created. The writer admonishes us to see that we not refuse Him that speaks from Heaven the way the Israelites refused Moses and, in their disobedience, died in the wilderness falling short of the promises and the reward. "Wherefore, holy brethren, partakers of the heavenly calling, consider the Apostle and High Priest of our profession, Christ Jesus, Who was faithful to him that appointed him, as also Moses was faithful in all his house" (Heb. 3:1-2 KJV). The Lord Jesus was God's chosen and appointed apostle to the world. He is also the last Adam sent to establish the Father's kingdom and reclaim the lost authority, dominion, and government forfeited by the first earthly man, Adam. The Father appoints faithful men such as Moses because, like Christ, he was found faithful among all those in the house of God.

Everything that the Father establishes in the earth is through covenant and promise, declaring that if you do this, He will do what He promised and agreed to. In everything the Father builds, He first appoints and establishes a foundation with those that He chooses to build with and then delegates to them His kingdom authority. It is through those heavenly ordered appointments that He calls, organizes, and structures a solid foundation for His people becoming firm and unchangeable. This high priestly ministry that Christ instituted, organized, and imparted to His disciples in His first coming is an unchangeable and eternal priesthood after the order of Melchizedek (see Neuhaus, J. [2016] *Melchizedek In Our Midst*).

Scripture References
Chapter Three

1 Pet. 1:5 Salvation and Deliverance
Ps 22:28, 31 A Seed Will Serve Him
Matt. 20:2-16 The Saints' Inheritance
Matt. 25:23 Concerning Loyalty and Faithfulness
Heb. 3:1-2 KJV Our Apostle and High Priest

Divine Patterns from Heaven

In a covenant ministered by angels through His mediator Moses, the Father in heaven left us a very exact and divine pattern to follow and imitate so that the work the Father has instituted in the earth will reproduce according to the pattern that was laid down. Moses was commanded to build God's house according to the pattern shown him in the holy mountain (Ex. 25:8-9). Jesus is the pattern Son and He is the living tabernacle. He calls us to follow Him as He leads us back to the Father's house and the place where the Father dwells in order that we may rest from our labors and find our final resting place in Him.

God, through Moses, created the Levite priesthood that contained two types of priests who served in the house, each with separate functions and different responsibilities. Though all the priesthood were from the tribe of Levi and set apart from other tribes, not all Levitical priests were high priests, which were called the *Cohanin*. This separation is important to comprehend if we are going to align ourselves in an ordered kingdom and government with the New Testament ministry of Melchizedek.

In the Old Covenant we have high priests chosen only from among Aaron and his sons. The office of the high priest and their service was to enter the most holy place with the welfare of the tribes of Israel upon their hearts, ministering before the Lord on their behalf, and ministering His Word and His Law to the people. The office of the Levite priest was not allowed to enter the Holy of Holies, their commission was to take care of the house and the vessels of the tabernacle which were a divine pattern and an example for the chosen offices of the New Testament. These chosen offices were given the commission to care for the living vessels and saints in God's house that are overseen by pastors, shepherds, and chosen ordained leaders.

One of the common errors of teaching that most of us have received is that this priesthood structure, created by covenant through Moses, has passed away, which could not be further from the truth. No, it did not pass away, it is permanent and still in operation through the high priestly ministry of Christ. The only thing that changed was the temporary high priestly ministry of Aaron which was done away with because it could not forever wash away sins, therefore, Aaron's high priestly ministry could not continue by reason of death.

The Old Covenant passed away and was replaced by the New Covenant that now operates in the earth through the high priestly ministry after the order of Melchizedek, which is an indestructible and eternal priesthood that ministers through the power of an endless life (Heb. 7:15-17). This truth is much more relevant now than ever before because in Christ we, as His kingdom priests, have been elevated in the earth through the new birth and the new covenant. "Now therefore, if ye will obey my voice indeed, and keep my covenant, then ye shall be a peculiar treasure unto me above all people: for all the earth is mine: And ye shall be unto me a kingdom of priests, and a holy nation. These are the words which thou shalt speak unto the children of Israel" (Ex. 19:5-6 KJV). The Father desired to have a kingdom of priests born from above, saints that would serve Him with the Law and the commandments written not on tables of stone but upon their hearts by the Spirit.

When Jesus came, He reinstated the order of Melchizedek and created a new high priestly order of ministry by establishing a company of kings and priests through His apostles, giving us written and experiential evidence that those He appointed operated as both kings and priests. According to Old Testament Law, Aaron could not operate in both offices at the same time. But now, with the same authority that the Father gave to Jesus, He also gave to His apostles, and when He breathed on them, He imparted the same power that the high priests in Israel had, which was to forgive sins or to retain sins. If the high priest of old said that you were still in your sins or had leprosy, a type of sin, that person retained their sins and remained unclean without argument, and if they had leprosy but were cleansed from their plague, the high priest would pronounce them clean. "Again, Jesus said, "Peace be with you! As the Father has sent me, I am sending you." And with that he breathed on them and said, "Receive the Holy Spirit. If you forgive anyone his sins, they are forgiven; if you do not forgive them, they are not forgiven" (John 20:21-24 NIV).

In the New Testament, Apostle Peter operated with the judgment of a king when he judged Ananias and Sapphira with the sentence of death, and he also operated as a priest when he and the other apostles received offerings, which only priests were to receive. Jesus reestablished the order of Melchizedek by appointing and anointing a chosen company of kings and priests. John, the apostle, claimed the king priest anointing when he stated, "to him that loved us and washed us in his own blood and has made us kings and priests to his God and Father"

(Rev. 1:5b, 6a). The book of Hebrews is a book of better things based on a better covenant and better promises declared to those Hebrew people that, concerning Melchizedek, there were many things to say, but the majority did not have ears to hear. In this generation, the Father is calling those that have an ear to hear the revelatory truths concerning the order of Melchizedek. For those that have ears to hear, the king priest ministry is operating in the earth today through those the Lord has chosen.

Scripture References
Chapter Four

Heb. 7:15-17 The Order of Melchizedek
Ex. 19:5-6 KJV A Peculiar Treasure
John 20:21-24 NIV I Am Sending You
Rev. 1:5b, 6a Kings and Priests

Wise Master Builders

When God's people arrive at the appointed times that the Father has set from the foundation of the world, He will first take from among men choice vessels to fulfill His Word and transition the church forward. The Apostle Paul was God's appointed and chosen vessel who almost singlehandedly pioneered and transitioned God's people from the age of the law to the age of grace. "But the Lord said unto him (Ananias), Go thy way: for he is a chosen vessel unto me, to bear my name before the Gentiles, and kings, and the children of Israel" (Acts 9:15 KJV). Any pioneer and chosen vessel of new truths and new things given to God's people must be prepared to endure hardship, rejection, persecutions, accusations, and defaming, from even their own brothers and those they once walked with. Paul experienced these things and still demonstrated in his life and ministry authentic apostleship and great humility. He was able to say, "Therefore I endure all things for the elect's sakes, that they may also obtain the salvation which is in Christ Jesus with eternal glory" (2 Tim. 2:10 KJV).

The Apostle Paul was an appointed steward in God's house, "Whereunto I am appointed a preacher, and an apostle, and a teacher of the Gentiles" (2 Tim. 1:11 KJV). He revealed that it was required in those that were stewards of the mysteries of God, called to oversee and manage the house of God, to be found faithful, "Let a man so consider us, as servants of Christ and stewards of the mysteries of God. Moreover, it is required in stewards that one be found faithful" (1 Cor. 4:1-2 NKJV).

JOHN NEUHAUS

The Apostle Paul was also a wise master builder, "According to the grace of God, which is given unto me, as a wise master builder, I have laid the foundation, and another buildeth thereon. But let every man take heed how he buildeth thereupon" (1 Cor. 3:10 KJV). As Jesus builds the kingdom the Father has entrusted to Him, there are chosen vessels that are masters and master builders. A wise master builder is a kingdom builder that is anointed with God's wisdom and one that knows how to build the church from the ground up in all of its aspects. A master is one that can read and comprehend the owner's plans and knows where everything fits in its proper position, placement, and order. In Paul's day, the apostle set order in all the churches revealing a pattern of how the kingdom works and how it operates according to God's divine purpose.

The Greek word for a master builder is *architekton*, which is an architect, the superintendent in the erection of buildings. One may declare he is an architect, but if they do not have the training and the appointment by God, they will most certainly build something that is inferior to what God is actually building. One of the great travesties in the church comes from those that presume they know how to build yet are not properly trained, anointed or equipped to build God's house. The Father's house cannot be properly built without those appointed to the task who have received, by revelation, the heavenly blueprints, and divine patterns. In the Church there are ministers who may be sincere, anointed, and mean well, yet are in truth not chosen to fulfill such a holy divine task and so, in the end, they will discover they were blind guides and all along building in vain which will often end up leading many to ruin and destruction.

Not many ministers are able to operate in all of God's fullness. In this day of fullness, God will once again set divine order among His people. A heavenly order will come to those that can hear what the Spirit is saying to the churches by raising up a remnant of anointed vessels to accomplish such a great undertaking that only the Father can perform. The Apostle Paul revealed that the body of Christ was a holy temple of sanctified, called out saints, called together as one, fitly framed and joined together, a body which would edify, build itself up, and grow up into a holy house, and people the Lord is pleased to dwell together with (Eph. 2:21, 4:16).

A word of caution to those that are seeking to build the house of God, you must with all diligence be careful how you build. If a man builds according to the foundation the Father has placed, which is Christ in conjunction with the apostles and prophets, the outcome will be much different from the one who doesn't build in line with this foundation (Eph. 3:20). All God's ministers must take heed how and what they build. If one builds a foundation with wood, hay, and stubble, revealing one that operates out of human plans, human knowledge and wisdom, and human effort, in the end these works shall be burned up in the judgment. Those ministers that build with gold, silver, and precious stones, revealing purified metals and jewels which have faithfully and truthfully withstood the fires of testing, will build God's house with heavenly wisdom according to heaven's plans and design. They will be proven qualified (1 Cor. 3:12-13 NIV). The fire of God's righteous judgments will test every man's work to prove the quality of their labor, whether or not it was built according to the Father's purposes in the earth. If a man's work abides the fire of God's testing, they will receive a reward and if a man's work fails the testing, his work shall be burned up and he will suffer loss, but he himself shall be saved though as by fire (1 Cor. 3:9, 15). In the day of the Lord's coming, all those that have built a true work for God, in the name of the Lord, will see their work manifested and plainly recognized for the day of the Lord will declare it.

Scripture References
Chapter Five

Acts 9:15 KJV Paul a Chosen Vessel
2 Tim. 2:10 KJV Enduring For the Elect's Sake
2 Tim. 1:11 KJV Paul An Appointed Steward
1 Cor. 4:1-2 NKJV Faithful Stewards
1 Cor. 3:10 KJV Take Heed How You Build
Eph. 2:21, 4:16 The Body of Christ
Eph. 3:20 Caution For Building
1 Cor. 3:12-13 NIV According to God's Design
1 Cor. 3:9, 15 Testing Through Fire

The Transitional Generation

At this present moment, God's people are living in a time of transition for the body of Christ. Not every generation is a transitional generation. God's people transition when a time of fullness has come and the church is ready to cross over and move from one season into a new season, which the Word of God calls set and appointed times. Transition in the church is a process of moving from an old and familiar place to a new and unfamiliar place almost always involving a way God's people have never been before. Concerning the body of Christ, transition always brings change; change of leadership, change of how the church operates, change of an age, and change of direction. Transition and change always begins with a revelation of the wisdom of God from heaven and an understanding of the times that is revealed to God's messengers and appointed men before that change processes and becomes a reality. The Father, every time, sends His messengers to prepare the way. He also sends us prophetic signs and warnings before a change or transition comes in order that God's people will be ready and prepared for the next season that the Father is bringing.

The prophets had been silent for four hundred years and then, just before the Son of God appeared, the Prophet Malachi prophesied, "See, I will send my messenger, who will prepare the way before me. Then suddenly the Lord you are seeking will come to his temple; the messenger of the covenant, whom you desire, will come, says the Lord Almighty" (Mal. 3:1-2 NIV). The Apostle Luke says, "This is he, of whom it is written, Behold, I send my messenger before thy face, which shall prepare thy way before thee" (Luke 7:27 KJV). In times past there may have only been a few messengers, yet for our day, we can expect more messengers because the call to prepare for the coming of the King and His kingdom is now global.

The Gospel of Luke tells us that the Lord sends messengers to make His people ready for His appearing in order that those, called by His name, will bring Him the honor and the glory that is rightfully His. And we, who love the truth, must make His paths straight and prepare the way for His coming. The Father says, "my thoughts are higher than your thoughts" and "my ways are not your ways" (Isa. 55:8). He desires the paths of His people and the way they walk to be according to His rule and authority that we may be upright in His sight and not dishonor His name (Luke 1:76, 3:4).

We know this is the generation that will receive the Lord and coronate Him as the rightful King to David's throne. The Father wants us to know His thoughts and His heart, and in this day, the Father is sending His messengers and prophets to tell us how to prepare for His second coming, which will be much different than His first coming. There are things we need to know in order to prepare for and understand the required paths we must follow. "Show me your ways, Lord, teach me your paths. Guide me in your truth and teach me, for you are God my Savior, and my hope is in you all day long" (Ps. 25:4-5 NIV).

Scripture References
Chapter Six

Mal. 3:1-2 NIV Malachi's Prophecy of Messiah
Luke 7:27 KJV My Messenger
Isa. 55:8 Prepare the Way
Luke 1:76, 3:4 His Rule and Authority
Ps. 25:4-5 NIV A Cry to God

Called and Appointed

In His first coming, Jesus laid down a pattern for us to follow concerning how He appoints those that are to lead His people into a new season and those that will govern His Church body during the coming kingdom age. Those that He chooses are those that have been called and appointed by Him even as the early apostles were called and trained personally by Jesus to operate as His leaders and government for their day. They were appointed by Him to lead the newly formed church that would arise through them. It was out of a multitude of many disciples that followed Jesus that He singled out and appointed the twelve. It is important to note that the first century apostles laid the foundation of the two-thousand-year Pentecostal church age and now, in the transition of our time, the newly appointed leaders and apostles of our day will lay the foundation for the age of the kingdom that will endure for a thousand years. This company, along with the patriarchs and the early apostles, will make up His governmental rule in the soon to be revealed kingdom age (Matt. 8:11).

In this hour, we will not escape if we refuse Him that speaks from heaven (Heb. 12:25). If one is to enter the kingdom age, it is imperative that we choose to be governed and to align ourselves and flow with the divine order and governmental structure that the Father is, at this time, establishing in the earth (Isa. 9:7). If we are to flow and work within the order and kingdom structure the Lord is setting up now, we will have to follow the Lord's proven and appointed leadership for this time. If one cannot flow with the Father's set order, one will not be able to flow in His kingdom. One might ask, "How are we going to find this set order of leadership that the Father is establishing in our generation?" It was through a heavenly revelation that the Apostle Paul, the Father's master builder, set the arrangement and spiritual order of the five-fold ministry of apostles, prophets, evangelists, pastors, and teachers. These divinely set offices were given for the perfecting of the saints, for the work of the ministry, and for building up the body of Christ. All of these ministry offices are functioning now, at the end of this age. The apostle reveals that these five offices will be in operation "until we all come into the unity of the faith" (Eph. 4:13).

The unifying of the faith must take place if we are to function as a kingdom people. Although we seem to have little unity in the body at this time, in reality it is taking place, though largely unseen and unnoticed as it was in the Lord's earthly ministry. In the Father's wisdom, God gives the keys of the kingdom and chooses people He can trust to rule and lead His body so as not to pollute the message of the kingdom with greedy and self-promoting men that will compromise the truths of heaven. Throughout the earth, the Lord is gathering together not only geographically, but spiritually, His remnant. His scattered remnant is being gathered together unto Him (2 Thess. 2:1).

The spiritually blind and unlearned will not see how the Father is unifying, fitly framing, and bringing together His body in the earth. The book of Acts reveals a divine pattern; the Lord first begins by choosing and setting in place His chosen appointed leaders, then afterwards, the formation of the body takes place and becomes united and connected to a company of unified spiritual leaders. This leads to what we see in the book of Acts; converts being added to the church daily. Truthfully, most leaders do not see the present forming of the Lord's kingdom government because it is a new thing not seen before and men love the old rather than the new in the same way that the grace of God was a new revelation to those that were under the Law in the time of the Apostle Paul. Jesus and Paul could not work with the religious system of their day, so the Father had to raise up new wine skins and form new leaders that were teachable and flexible enough to obey Him and follow Him.

What must happen in the body of Christ for us to see and hear accurately? The early church entered a new season with a small group of future leaders that came together with one mind and one heart and as they waited upon the Lord, this remnant company of 120 faithful disciples were the first to be sealed with the Holy Spirit of promise from heaven. Afterward, the Holy Spirit was poured out upon all flesh and many people were joined to the Lord. A unified leadership is integral in order for God's people to move into a new day, no matter how small and insignificant it may seem.

Is the body of Christ going to come into unity of the faith as the apostle said we would and become one as Jesus and the Father are one and for which Jesus prayed? What is impossible with man is possible with God (Luke 18:27). We, all that believe, must now strive, and contend for the truths of our faith if we are to enter that straight and narrow gate that leads to His life (Matt. 7:14). Secondarily, we must be doers of the Word and not hearers only (Jas. 1:22) for only those that obey and do the Word will be justified and made righteous with the ability to live and walk in the righteousness that it takes to become the Father's kingdom saints. If a believer only hears the Word and yet does not do it or obey the Word, will that believer be justified? It is certain that one that does not obey the Word of God will not be doing the will of the Father, for the kingdom only comes when we, His people, do the will of God on the earth as it is done in heaven. All in heaven do the will of the Father. So, the question remains, will the person that does not obey be counted worthy to enter the kingdom age? Jesus said, "not everyone that says Lord will enter the kingdom but only those that do the will of the Father in heaven" (Matt. 7:21). The reader of this book must answer that question for themselves.

Scripture References
Chapter Seven

Matt. 8:11 Reclining at the Kingdom's Table
Heb. 12:25 Those Who Refuse Him That Speaks
Isa. 9:7 Earth's Divine Order
Eph. 4:13 The Unity of the Faith
2 Thess. 2:1 The Remnant
Luke 18:27 Possible With God
Jas. 1:22 Doers of the Word
Matt. 7:22 The Will of the Father

The Blowing of Trumpets

It is important to God that His people receive warnings, such as the blowing of the trumpet in Zion that acted as an alarm to His people. Trumpets were blown before potential trouble came so that the people could prepare and be ready. From the time of Moses onward, in the nation of Israel, trumpets were used to get the attention of the people. The trumpets were blown by the Levitical priests, not everyone was appointed to blow the trumpet, which makes us all subject to hear from chosen leadership. The trumpet blasts were a clarion call for all the people to hear. Two silver trumpets, revealing redemption, were used for the gathering, and assembling of all the separate tribes and for giving the people direction concerning how they were to move forward. If there was only one trumpet sounded, the leaders were to gather to Moses. Each blast had a different meaning; a call for the entire congregation to gather, a call for the leadership to gather, or a call to battle. "And the Lord spoke to Moses, saying: "Make two silver trumpets for yourself; you shall make them of hammered work; you shall use them for calling the congregation and for directing the movement of the camps. When they blow both of them, all the congregation shall gather before you at the door of the tabernacle of meeting. But if they blow *only* one, then the leaders, the heads of the divisions of Israel, shall gather to you. When you sound the advance, the camps that lie on the east side shall then begin their journey. When you sound the advance the second time, then the camps that lie on the south side shall begin their journey; they shall sound the call for them to begin their journeys. And when the assembly is to be gathered together, you shall blow, but not sound the advance. The sons of Aaron, the priests, shall blow the trumpets; and these shall be to you as an ordinance forever throughout your generations" (Num.10:1-8 NKJV).

The trumpets were made of pure silver hammered and molded into shape by fire and testing. Those that the Father uses to lift up their voice like a trumpet must be perfected in order that they may bring forth a pure and true sound. To New Covenant people, the message of our redemption comes by way of prophetic impartations and warnings from appointed leadership. The Father said to the prophet Isaiah, "Cry aloud, spare not; Lift up your voice like a trumpet; Tell My people their transgression, And the house of Jacob their sins" (Isa. 58:1 NKJV). A transgression is one that goes against the rule or set order of a thing by walking contrary to the council and warnings that the Father sends through His messengers. God, in His mercy, wants His people to know their sins and shortcomings that we might repent and turn towards Him with all of our hearts. In the New Testament we also receive some serious warnings. We have messengers and prophets, like John the Baptist, that warned the nation and the spiritual leaders to repent and flee from the wrath and judgment to come. The consequences for rejecting those that were sent were high and very costly. Because the nation of Israel and its leaders rejected God's heavenly sent messengers and the message of redemption and forgiveness that Jesus preached, He said the kingdom would be taken from them and given to a nation that would bring forth the fruits of salvation.

Christ in us is the hope that at the end of our earthly lives we will enter into His glorious kingdom with the angels and the saints of all ages, a time when every person will be presented to Christ holy and complete. "To whom God would make known what is the riches of the glory of this mystery among the Gentiles; which is Christ in you, the hope of glory: whom we preach, warning every man, and teaching every man in all wisdom; that we may present every man perfect in Christ Jesus" (Col. 1:27-29 KJV). God's people do not always know the times when the Father is moving them forward, it is, however, being revealed to the apostles and prophets by the Spirit (Eph. 3:5). Some do not hear what the Father is saying because they are not listening to the right people. There are many voices that are speaking bad, false, or enticing messages, sounding brass and tinkling cymbals. They are with vain and empty words and no revelation for the coming season. The Apostle John said, "many false prophets and teachers have gone out into the world" (1 John 4:1).

True prophets are not always popular so we, as His people, must first seek the Lord and then we must, with utmost prayer and discernment, seek out the true prophets and spiritually mature fathers of our time. The Apostle Paul declared that we are not in darkness that we should miss the day or timing of the Lord's coming (1 Thess. 5:4). The body of Christ in this present hour has come to an appointed time, yet many and even most of God's people do not perceive or discern the time or the requirements that the Lord is calling for in order for us to be prepared. The messengers the Father sends will tell us how we need to prepare. God wants us to know how His kingdom is coming, how it will manifest, and who the true leaders are, those that the Father has chosen to prepare us to enter the coming age. "Even the stork in the sky knows her appointed seasons, and the dove, the swift and the thrush observe the time of their migration. But my people do not know the requirements of the Lord" (Jer. 8:7-8 NIV).

JOHN NEUHAUS

Scripture References
Chapter Eight

Num.10:1-8 NKJV The Silver Trumpets
Isa. 58:1 NKJV Voice like a Trumpet
Col. 1:27-29 KJV Holy and Complete
Eph. 3:5 God's Times Revealed
1 John 4:1 False Prophets
1 Thess. 5:4 Not in Darkness
Jer. 8:7-8 NIV Knowing God's Times

The Last Generation

"For unto us a child is born, unto us a son is given: and the government shall be upon his shoulder" (Isa. 9:6 KJV). In our day it will not be the high priestly ministry of Aaron and his sons that lead us to the place of our eternal rest, it will be Jesus, our eternal High Priest after the order of Melchizedek, and His appointed sons and representative government that will shoulder and lead the people in the kingdom age. The writer to the Hebrews states concerning Melchizedek, "Of whom we have many things to say but you are slow to hear" (Heb. 5:11). There are many things that now need to be said concerning the heavenly order of Melchizedek. The Father has chosen this hour for us to hear that we might learn His government and how it operates in order that we might have a sure entrance into the kingdom age that is quickly coming forth in the earth. The sons and daughters appointed to the order of Melchizedek will be Israelites chosen from among the nations and peoples of this generation that will arise as a holy priesthood leading a holy people who will be called sons of the kingdom. God knows those that are His and is even now, at the end of the age, cleansing His threshing floor and separating the children of the kingdom from the children of the wicked one; the wheat from the chaff, separating the hypocrites, the profane, and the sinners of His people from among the righteous and the holy (Matt. 3:12, 13:38).

In the Lord's first coming, He came seeking fruit from a fig tree that represented the nation of Israel, His covenant people, and He found none. He was quick to curse it for not bearing fruit. Now, in our day, so much testimony and revelation has been given to us and the Lord is once again seeking fruit from this generation. In this hour, many Christian church systems are broken and, like Israel of old, they cannot produce the fruit the Father is looking for or build a spiritual house that He is pleased to dwell in. Joshua's day was a pattern of divinely appointed leadership that will arise in this day with a high priestly ministry bearing the government of Christ on their shoulders exhorting His people that when we see a priesthood bearing the presence of God, we are to move from our place and where ever it might be follow after it that we may know the way. In this hour we will only know the way when we follow authentic ministry ordained by God and not by man. "For not he who commends himself is approved, but whom the Lord commends" (2 Cor. 10:18 NKJV).

At the first coming of Christ, God's people transitioned to a new age called the church age and the new season began with a great outpouring of the Holy Spirit. At that time many words of the prophets were fulfilled, yet numerous prophetic words and warnings were not heeded by many of the Lord's people and the whole nation of Israel missed the time of their visitation (Luke 19:44). Before the second coming of Christ, the Lord will send us prophets, apostles, and wise men to warn us of things to come, but sadly many will follow the ways of Israel that took no serious heed in the time of Jesus and will also miss the necessary preparations required to move forward to the next season (Luke 11:49). We must be as the wise virgins that prepared for the Lord's coming beforehand in case, they had to walk through the darkness to meet the Lord (Matt. 25:1-13). We must take notice of God's messengers and prepare, in order that we will be found worthy to escape the great judgments coming upon the world and be able to stand before the Son of Man, for the judgments of God will fall swiftly upon those that know not God and do not obey the gospel (2 Thess. 1:8). "Watch ye therefore, and pray always, that ye may be accounted worthy to escape all these things that shall come to pass, and to stand before the Son of man" (Luke 21:36 KJV).

Through the prophets, the gospels, and the epistles, many future things were prophesied concerning the last generation, prophecies that will be fulfilled just prior to the Lord's return and His coming in the clouds of heaven with power and great glory. In His great end-time discourse, Jesus gave us the sign of the final generation when all things that are written will be fulfilled. He told us that when you see Israel, God's fig tree nation, blossom, His coming will be very near, even at the doors, and that generation will not pass until all the things He has said come to pass. He told us that false prophets and false christs with false anointings will arise and deceive many, not just a few. In His prophetic discourse, Jesus said this gospel of the kingdom would be preached in all the world, not just to win more souls, but as a witness to the whole world and then the end would come. This gospel of the coming kingdom is being proclaimed now to those that have ears to hear.

Not everyone is willing to change from the old, the familiar, and the comfortable to the new and unfamiliar. The great challenge to this present generation is, are we willing to go in a way we have never been? Are we willing to be instructed by spiritual fathers and led by God-appointed leadership rather than ten thousand instructors? God was angry with a whole generation of people that would not obey His appointed leaders and swore that they would not enter the land and receive any of His good promises. "Therefore, just as the Holy Spirit says, 'today if you hear his voice,' do not harden your hearts as when they provoked me, as in the day of trial in the wilderness, where your fathers tried me by testing me, and saw my works for forty years. therefore, I was angry with this generation, and said, they always go astray in their heart, and they did not know my ways; as I swore in my wrath, 'they shall not enter my rest'" (Heb. 3:7-12 NASU).

The last generation is a chosen generation and royal priesthood that the Father has prepared for such a time as this, a people that will experience the greatest transition the earth has ever seen. This is the prophesied final generation that will pass over into the land of God's promises and inherit the earth forever (Ps. 37:29, 34). In this day, as in the days of old, God will raise up spiritual Joshua's that will lead us through this great transition and bring us into our resting place in Christ. In this day of trouble and tribulation, the Father will send deliverers and anointed apostles and prophets upon mount Zion, the place of God's rule; overcomers, and chief men and women that will have authority over the nations ruling them with a shepherd's rod of iron. All of creation is eagerly anticipating the manifestation of the sons of God that will set creation free and deliver God's people into the glorious liberating power of the sons of God (Rom. 8:19). The key principle of transition for our generation will be for the people of God to know the difference between the holy and the unholy or profane and follow the true leadership, a Zadok type priesthood that the Father has appointed in this generation.

"And they shall teach My people *the difference* between the holy and the unholy, and cause them to discern between the unclean and the clean" (Ezek. 44:23 NKJV).

Scripture References
Chapter Nine

Isa. 9:6 KJV A Son Is Given
Heb. 5:11 About Melchizedek
Matt. 3:12, 13:38 God's Threshing Floor
2 Cor. 10:18 NKJV Those Whom the Lord Commends
Luke 19:44 Israel's Time of Visitation
Luke 11:49 Take Heed to Prepare
Matt. 25:1-13 Wise Virgins
2 Thess. 1:8 Found Worthy
Luke 21:36 KJV Watch and Pray
Heb. 3:7-12 NASU God's Rest
Ps. 37:29, 34 Those Who Inherit
Rom. 8:19 Manifestation of the Sons of God
Ezek. 44:23 NKJV Clean and Unclean

Appointed Ones

Those that are chosen vessels, anointed and appointed by the Father and the Son to transition the people of God, come with new revelation for a new season for the church. These will begin to say what few are saying, they have been given divine authority authenticated with signs and wonders. The Apostle Paul declared that the gospel of grace was his gospel and that he was a wise master builder or an architect with a heavenly sent blueprint given to him for that season. If it were not for the Apostle Paul, the church would not know grace, we would not have a revelation of communion, even though the other apostles broke bread together with Jesus they gave no revelation concerning communion, and last but not least, he gave us a divinely ordained structure for the church with apostles as the first, prophets, evangelists, pastors, and teachers.

Though Apostle Paul was a chosen vessel, he went up and submitted himself to the chiefest of the apostles that were before him to communicate with them, honoring them, and receiving their blessing in order that he might not have run in vain with what God gave him by revelation. He shared his revelations and received their blessing with some instruction. We all should be very careful and cautious with appointed men, honoring them, because in their appointment from heaven they come equipped and sent with a word from God and the judgment of kings in their mouths. We must keep in mind that no matter how humble and unpretentious those sent by God might be, to reject or refuse them either willingly, proudly, or even in ignorance, will eventually find you rejecting the Father Himself (Matt. 10:40; John 13:20).

This writing is purposed to show the difference between those that have been appointed by the Lord to lead His people into the next age and those that may be anointed yet have not been chosen or appointed by the Father. In the days to come, it will be important and vital to see the difference between those that have been chosen and appointed versus those that are anointed. All true ministers should be anointed but not all are appointed. The great mistake that many leaders will make is that because they are anointed, and may even be very successful in ministry, they will think they are His appointed leaders also. This is not so and will cause many to follow a false and counterfeit governmental church system that often will operate in error and false teaching. Even though they may be good leaders and love the Lord, they will have taken a position that is not rightfully theirs and a position they are not appointed to fulfill, such leaders have presumptuously taken the highest seats of the House of God that do not belong to them. This book is intended to challenge long-held mindsets and traditions that many have held to. The way to enter into life is still narrow and very few there are that find it (Matt. 7:13-14).

Scripture References
Chapter Ten
Matt. 10:40 Submission to Proper Authority
John 13:20 He Who Receives Me
Matt. 7:13-14 Narrow Is the Way

We Have Never Been This Way Before

The book of Joshua and the entrance into the Promised Land was a divine pattern and type of God's people entering the kingdom age. Because the people did not fully conquer the land, the writer to the Hebrews tells us of another day when God's people would fully occupy the land and enter the kingdom age. At that time, the Lord's enemies will be defeated by Jesus, the Captain of the Lord's armies, and His loyal and believing saints. "For if Joshua had given them rest, He would not have spoken of another day. So there remains a Sabbath rest for the people of God" (Heb. 4:8-9 NASU).

Joshua commanded the officers and the officers commanded and gave direction to the people about entering in. "Then Joshua rose early in the morning; and he and all the sons of Israel set out from Shittim and came to the Jordan, and they lodged there before they crossed. At the end of three days the officers went through the midst of the camp; and they commanded the people, saying, 'When you see the ark of the covenant of the Lord your God with the Levite priests carrying it, then you shall set out from your place and go after it. However, there shall be between you and it a distance of about 2,000 cubits by measure. Do not come near it, that you may know the way by which you shall go, for you have not passed this way before'" (Josh. 3:1-5 NASU). The priesthood that carried the ark on their shoulders were not ordinary priests, they were the high priests called the *Cohanin*, they were the sons of Aaron. Isaiah 9:6 says, "For unto us a child is born, unto us a son is given: and the government shall be upon his shoulder." The government of Christ will be the high priestly Melchizedek order and ministry that the Lord has appointed to shoulder, and bear on their hearts, the responsibility of God's people bearing heavenly rule in the now rising kingdom of God.

In our day, when we see an appointed and anointed priesthood leading God's people into the kingdom age, we are to move from any fixed position and follow them. The trumpet alarm has been sounded; God is calling all of His leaders in the five-fold ministry to respond to the official authorities that are shouldering His government in the earth, those He has chosen to lead us into the kingdom in order that the people they shepherd will also follow (Num. 10:1-8). If we are to know the way into the kingdom, we must follow what the Father has appointed for us, for we have never been this way before.

The church is moving into new territory, a way we as God's people have never experienced. The Father left us a divine pattern of the kingdom age when Joshua commanded the people to stand back two thousand spaces from the ark of the covenant, which was a measured prophetic timeline of two thousand cubits revealing that God's people and final generation would not enter the kingdom age until two thousand years from the time of Christ, that is exactly where we are today. We, the church, have now fulfilled the season of Pentecost that has lasted for two thousand years, and the end of that season has come as an appointed priesthood arises to lead the people of God into their final resting place in the kingdom of Christ, fulfilling the Father's promises in us, to us, and through us.

The generation that came out of the wilderness in Joshua's time did not fully possess the Promised Land, yet it foreshadowed and pictured a future day when God's people, led by the Lord Jesus, the Captain of God's armies, will together defeat all of Christ's enemies and take the kingdom under the whole heaven. Joshua, a son and a loyal disciple of Moses, a master prophet, shepherd, and administrator, reveals a divine pattern of the coming kingdom age that will take place just before the Lord's return. The Hebrew writer tells us that Joshua was not able to bring the people of God into their final resting place, but that it will be fulfilled and happen in a future day, which is our day.

Scripture References
Chapter Eleven
Heb. 4:8-9 NASU There Remains a Rest
Josh. 3:1-5 NASU Carrying the Ark
Num. 10:1-8 Calling the Assembly

God's Government

God's people are standing at the door of a new day, but before Christ returns to be seated upon the throne of His father David. The prophet Daniel reveals to us a precise prophetic timeline concerning the end of days when the God of heaven will set up and form a kingdom that will not be given to other people but will be given to the saints of the Most High, a time when judgment will be assigned to the saints and they shall possess the kingdom under the whole heaven (Dan. 2:44, 7:22-27). The Lord even tells Daniel that he would stand in his allotted place at the end of days (Dan.12:13).

It is in the days and time of the rise of the antichrist and his system that the ten kings that have no kingdom, as of yet, will give their power to the beast for one hour, which in spiritual time is forty-two months, that the God of heaven will order and organize His kingdom. He will set it up and arrange it with a chosen and prequalified priesthood that He, personally, will appoint and train to lead His people into our next season. This is an appointed time and a new day for the church that comes with new operations, higher dimensions, and revelations of the truths of God's Word. The Lord will raise up a company of overcoming sons and daughters that have been granted to sit with Him in His Father's throne and they will be given authority over the nations and will rule them with a shepherd's rod. To the overcomer, Jesus will give the morning star, which is the first light out of the darkness of this world (Rev. 2:26-27, 3:21).

In the book of Acts a new thing and a fulfilled promise never seen before was revealed from heaven when God sent power from on high and all were filled with the Holy Spirit. Heavenly ordained transitions always come with new leadership and new ways of operating. Rest assured that this final transition will come with power and new leadership and the Father will not ask us if we agree with it. The group of twelve that Jesus called and prepared were chosen and specially appointed along with seventy other disciples and chosen women that became the one hundred and twenty loyal, committed, and unified disciples; the chosen saints that moved the people of God into a new day.

Even when the new thing from God was moving forward and being established with great signs and wonders, the old religious order continued as always doing their animal sacrifices, even after the great sacrifice of God's own Son who was rejected, ignored, scoffed at, and finally crucified; a monumental event the whole city of Jerusalem knew about but chose to ignore and fight against. The spiritually blind continued to lead the blind with force and cruelty and the old leadership that refused to move or submit to God's new leaders led a whole nation down the path of destruction and into the pit of ruin and desolation. After the crucifixion and ascension of Jesus, God gave the nation of Israel a season of mercy to repent and then forty years after the time of Jesus, the old religious order with its rebellious priesthood and nation was judged by God, destroyed, and left desolate because they knew not the time when God visited their nation (Luke 19:44).

In this season, the Lord is appointing men among His people to positions of His newly formed government; men and women that will lead His people into the next age. Many of those that He is appointing are unknown and unseen, like the first disciples of Christ, they are His hidden ones that He has entrusted to prepare His bride for His return. These chosen ones are trusted by God and will not by any means defile or pollute the Lord's bride with lies or falsehoods. All of creation is now in pain and travail waiting for the manifestation of the sons of God who will free the earth from all bondage and corruption bringing together all of His people into the glorious liberty of His sons and daughters (Rom. 8:19, 22).

Scripture References
Chapter Twelve

Dan. 2:44, 7:22-27 Daniel's prophetic timeline
Dan. 12:13 Daniel's Allotted Place
Rev. 2:26-27, 3:21 He Who Overcomes
Luke 19:44 The Time of God's Visitation
Rom. 8:19, 22 Creation Groans

Three Major Set Times in the Feasts of Israel

In the Old Covenant there are three major feasts that the Israelites were commanded to keep. The keeping of these feasts was recorded for us as a divine pattern revealing the exact set times and seasons that the church would pass through on her way to the perfect or mature day (Prov. 4:18). Through these three feasts and appointed times held every year in Israel, we can trace the seasons and calculate the church's progressive movement forward all the way to the final generation that will be born just before Jesus returns. Soon what Jesus taught us to pray will be answered and we will say, "Thy kingdom has come, and thy will is now being done, in the earth as it is in heaven" (Matt. 6:10). The Law and journeys of Israel were a shadow and a preview of the good things that have come to us in Christ under the New Covenant (Heb. 10:1).

In the Tabernacle the court of Passover measured 1500 cubits and corresponds to the age of the law from Moses to Jesus, which is 1500 years. The inner court of Pentecost measured 2000 cubits and corresponds to the Church's age of grace and visitation that has lasted now for 2000 years beginning with the apostles to this final generation. At this time, an appointed government will keep the last and final feast, the Feast of Tabernacles, which reveals the holy of holies that measured 1000 cubits, corresponding to the one-thousand-year age of the kingdom that all resurrected saints will fulfill for the next thousand years as they rule and reign, together with Christ, as joint heirs. After the final feast is completed, we will have a new heaven and a new earth as the world that we once knew goes into eternity.

The Lord's gracious dealings, and sometimes severe chastisements, that natural Israel passed through, were given as examples for our instruction and learning that in the fullness of time the Lord would prepare a seed to serve Him in the kingdom age. "These things happened to them as examples and were written down as warnings for us, on whom the end of the ages has come. So, if you think you are standing firm, be careful that you don't fall" (1 Cor. 10:11-12 NIV)!

Isaiah tells us that through his seed, the Messiah would prolong his days and extend his ministry of righteousness in the earth and the pleasure of the Lord, that which is acceptable in the Father's eyes, would prosper in his hand through his sacrificial work. In the last days a generation will arise that the Lord of the harvest will be pleased to dwell with and not be ashamed to call them his brethren (Isa. 53:10). "A seed shall serve him; it shall be accounted to the Lord for a generation. They shall come and shall declare his righteousness unto a people that shall be born, that he had done *this*" (Ps. 22:30-31 KJV). This is the seed of the woman that will bruise the head of Satan. The people that shall come will declare His righteousness as they follow the 144,000 first-fruits company who stand with the Lamb upon Mount Zion where God has set His king along with the Lord's high priestly first-fruits company chosen after the order of Melchizedek (Ps. 2:6; Rev. 12:1-5). It is important to note a scripture that most theologians fail to recognize which is the divine and set order of the resurrection revealing to us that every man will be raised in his own order or company and the first to be raised from the dead are the first-fruits company of God (Rev. 14:1-5 KJV). "For as in Adam all die, even so in Christ shall all be made alive. But every man in his own order: Christ the first fruits; afterward they that are Christ's at his coming. Then cometh the end, when he shall have delivered up the kingdom to God, even the Father; when he shall have put down all rule and all authority and power. For he must reign, till he hath put all enemies under his feet" (1 Cor. 15:22-26 KJV).

Scripture References
Chapter Thirteen

Prov. 4:18 The Path of the Just
Matt. 6:10 Thy Kingdom Come
Heb. 10:1 A Shadow
1 Cor. 10:11-12 NIV Take Heed
Isa. 53:10 He Shall See His Seed
Ps. 22:30-31 KJV A Seed Shall Serve Him
Ps. 2:6 My King On Zion
Rev. 12:1-5 One to Rule All Nations
Rev. 14:1-5 First Fruits to God
1 Cor. 15:22-26 Resurrection Order

The Three Major Transitions of God's People

The first major transition of God's people came in the time of the Passover. The Hebrew people were a tribal people that would come under Egyptian bondage and great affliction, but God promised Abraham that He would deliver His people (Gen. 15:13-14). God raised up Moses as their deliverer in order that they could worship the Lord in the wilderness and receive the Law from Moses. He was their God-sent and appointed leader as well as a shepherd who guided and led them through their wilderness journey. Moses's commission from God was to lead this newly formed nation out of bondage and into the land promised to Abraham and his descendants. By the hand of Moses, the Father gave them righteous laws and judgments, but under trial and test in the wilderness, the people rebelled against God's chosen leader and, with many of them, God was not well pleased. They were overthrown in the wilderness and never obtained the promise of their inheritance or possessed the land flowing with milk and honey (1 Cor. 10:5). The writer to the Hebrews warns us to take heed to this example lest there be in any of us an evil heart of unbelief and we fall short of the promises left to us, failing to enter our promised land, the kingdom age (Heb. 3:12).

The second major transition happened when God's people moved from the age of the law to the age of grace. From the day the New Testament church was birthed at Pentecost, the people of God began to completely operate in a new and life-giving way with a divinely appointed and completely new leadership. The old religious order gave way to the new order and with the new came divine change, yet all that heard did not transition and all were not ready or willing to change and move forward or recognize the new leadership the Father had formed on the day of Pentecost. The old religious order had decayed and become harsh and legalistic whereby it became obsolete without any redemptive power to deliver, and it faded away (Heb. 8:13). The old system of righteous laws that God established in the beginning had become corrupted with little righteousness in it. The leaders of Jesus's day, whom He called murderers and hypocrites, had corrupted God's way and the priesthood structure that was pure and holy in its beginning. They now had the spirit of Cain, condemning and murdering the most just, operating with controlling legalism and traditions that made the Word of God ineffective and powerless to rightly teach, influence, and lead God's people in the paths of righteousness. A once faithful city and people prostituted themselves for unjust gain, power, and money called filthy lucre (Isa. 1:21, 23).

Grace and truth came by Jesus Christ. Although the gospel of the grace of God was a mystery not yet revealed and hidden from other ages by God's sovereign choice, the full teaching of grace was given to the Apostle Paul by revelation as were other hidden truths revealed to him by the Spirit (Eph. 3:1-5). The Father chose one man that transitioned God's people from the age of the law to the age of grace. It was the Apostle Paul, an apostle specially born for the season of grace, a chosen vessel to dispense this great doctrine of divine truth, that almost single handedly moved the people that had ears to hear in that day from the age of the law to the new season of grace. This transition did not happen overnight and took, at the least, a full generation for men to receive this new teaching that Paul was commissioned by God to dispense, which the apostle called his gospel, the gospel of the grace of God (Eph. 3:2; Rom. 2:16). It took a revelation and a knowledge of the mysteries of the kingdom given by the Holy Spirit and written in the canon of scripture for men to comprehend and enter the age of grace. It will also take a revelation of the Holy Spirit for men to enter the kingdom age. One may learn grace by diligent study, but in order for one to transition into kingdom order and kingdom living, it comes by way of instruction and discipleship (Matt. 13:52 KJV).

The Father established the governmental office of the apostle first and He will in this last time once again bring forth a company of last day apostles keeping to the truth Jesus taught us that "the first would be last and the last would be first" (Matt. 20:16). The early apostles laid the foundation and teaching for the age of Pentecost and now, as we prepare to enter the age of the kingdom, the Father is already choosing out from among men a pre-qualified priesthood to lead and instruct His people into this next season. Keep in mind that the Lord's kingdom and His government will continue to increase and prosper for a thousand years (Isa. 9:7). As it was during the time of Jesus, much of this new leadership is unknown and unseen. The great question is, are people going to see this new kingdom order before it appears, or will it be only a small remnant as it was in the early church? We must keep in mind that Jesus said that the kingdom began with the least and smallest of seeds but when it was planted, it grew into a great tree that spread out great branches.

People tend to look upon that which is great and noble rather than that which is least and seemingly insignificant, none expected the Messiah to choose and groom His leadership from common men which caused many to stumble and many to reject. The leaders and elders of Christ's day were looking for a noble king to deliver them from their enemies but instead got a humble servant, a sacrificial lamb, and in their self-righteous presumption they wandered away from truth and virtue and erred, not knowing the scriptures or the power of God (Matt. 22:29). The Pharisees, who were noted to be experts in the Word of God, fell into serious error and led many who trusted in them to stray from Jesus, their true shepherd and king. The Father sets believers in the body as He sees fit and as believers, we are required to be joined to the body of Christ, so it is imperative that we seek the Lord for the place that He desires to put us in the body. Believers are also required to submit themselves to their leaders, yet in this day we must also be discerning for everything is not always as good as it may appear. When we have diligently sought the Lord and are sure where the Father has placed us in His body, we will have peace and assurance that we are in the right place. We must hear and keep the word of the kingdom and keep it without compromise. When the Father does a new thing in the earth, we as His people are responsible to discern the times and the seasons that the Father has kept in His own power, ready to be revealed in the last time. God's people are crossing the threshold of a new day and, though it be only a remnant, there will be a first-fruits company that will be raised first, and like the book of Acts, the rest will follow (Joel 2:32).

Let each believer and each leader be assured that in this final generation the Lord is now forming His coming government and, like no other day before us, in this day the Father will have a functioning government prepared for His people, which will be set before He returns to take up His rightful throne. We must each choose to seek the Lord for this new leadership and transition to the new changes that are coming to the church ready and prepared to be revealed in the last time to His apostles and prophets by the Spirit. The Father purposed the New Testament and the gospels to be a natural type and similitude of the day we live in which has been given to us as a divine pattern of how to transition from the old to the new. One can choose to follow the blind into destruction or seek God for the who's who of His kingdom which will be made manifest more and more as the day of His return grows closer.

The last generation is a chosen generation and royal priesthood that the Father has prepared for such a time as this, a people that will experience the greatest transition the earth has ever seen. This is the prophesied final generation that will pass over into the land of God's promises and inherit the land forever (Ps. 37:29, 34). When transitions come, they bring change. The key principle of transition is that if God's people do not obey, believe, and follow the leadership that the Father has appointed in their generation, they will fall short of the mark of the high calling of God in Christ. In this hour we must press into the kingdom through all the lies and unbelief in the world in order that we, as His chosen people, receive a full reward and the fulfillment of what the Father has promised to His children in His Word (2 John 1:8 KJV).

Scripture References
Chapter Fourteen

Gen. 15:13-14 God's Promise to Deliver

1 Cor. 10:5 God was not pleased

Heb. 3:12 Take Heed

Heb. 8:13 A New Covenant

Isa. 1:21, 23 A Warning

Eph. 3:1-5 Paul's Revelation

Eph. 3:2 Stewardship of God's Grace

Rom. 2:16 Paul's Gospel

Matt. 13:52 KJV Kingdom Scribes

Matt. 13:52 The First Will Be Last

Isa. 9:7 The Lord's Government

Matt. 22:29 The Scriptures and the Power of God

Joel 2:32 He Who Calls on the Name of the Lord

Ps. 37:29, 34 The Righteous Shall Inherit

2 John 1:8 KJV A Warning to Watch

Be Ready

Many believe what the angels said when Jesus was taken up in a cloud, "Men of Galilee, why do you stand looking into the sky? This Jesus, who has been taken up from you into heaven, will come in just the same way as you have watched Him go into heaven" (Acts 1:11 NASU). Jesus is coming in the clouds of heaven with His holy angels, so we must not be deceived or caught unaware of His coming. Jesus tells us that He is coming at an hour we don't expect, and He also cautions us to be dressed, ready to move, and like men that are waiting for their master when he returns, ready to open the door to him immediately, welcoming him in without fear or guilt. We must be alert and awake, full of the oil of the Holy Spirit working in our lives, and even if He comes in the second or third watch, be prepared to meet the Lord at any moment.

We should watch and be aware of the Lord's coming the same way we would watch and guard our house if we knew the hour a thief was coming to break in (Matt. 24:43). These are solemn warnings that we should give our whole attention to, for many are not ready and are not preparing for His return. The Word of God tells us in many places how to be ready and how we then should live. "Be very careful, then, how you live—not as unwise but as wise making the most of every opportunity, because the days are evil. Therefore, do not be foolish, but understand what the Lord's will is. Do not get drunk on wine, which leads to debauchery. Instead, be filled with the Spirit. Speak to one another with psalms, hymns, and spiritual songs. Sing and make music in your heart to the Lord, always giving thanks to God the Father for everything, in the name of our Lord Jesus Christ" (Eph. 5:15-20 NIV).

Many preach and think they know the time of the Lord's coming and when His bride will be taken out of this world, but for the most part it is mere conjecture, suppositions, and fabrications of the mind not based on the Word of God with no heaven-sent revelation for the season. "Stay dressed for action and keep your lamps burning and be like men who are waiting for their master to come home from the wedding feast, so that they may open the door to him at once when he comes and knocks. Blessed are those servants whom the master finds awake when he comes. Truly, I say to you, he will dress himself for service and have them recline at table, and he will come and serve them. If he comes in the second watch, or in the third, and finds them awake, blessed are those servants! But know this, that if the master of the house had known at what hour the thief was coming, he would not have left his house to be broken into. You also must be ready for the Son of Man is coming at an hour you do not expect" (Luke 12:35-40 ESV).

The wise virgins, with much diligence and forethought, prepared for the bridegroom's return beforehand, revealing a company of wise saints that worshipped the Lord in spirit and in truth. The virgins identify themselves as true worshippers with plenty of oil in their vessels enabling them to see the way and light their paths through the darkness of this world. The foolish virgins did not prepare for the coming darkness and took no oil with them, not realizing they needed to buy the truth and sell it without compromise. We must make sure our vessels are filled with the Holy Spirit to light our way. When the bridegroom returned at midnight, the darkest hour of the day, a cry went out to go out to meet him and the wise arose and trimmed their wicks, which represents the care we must take in preparing our spiritual lives to be in order to meet the master. At the time it was needed the most, the lamps of the foolish and careless virgins went out and, therefore, they had no light within them from the Holy Spirit to guide them through the darkness of this world to meet the Lord.

The foolish virgins asked the wise virgins to give them oil to which they said they couldn't because there was not enough for both of them and if they did, because of the foolish virgins' choices and lack of preparation, the wise virgins would fail to find their way through the darkness to meet the bridegroom. The wise virgins told them to go and buy oil for themselves. When the foolish virgins went to buy oil, it was too late, the bridegroom had already come and those that were ready went into the marriage and the door into the kingdom age was shut. The foolish virgins came to the house still believing they would be able to enter, but the door to God's house was closed. They pleaded with the master to please open the door, but the master answered and said, "I know you not" (Matt. 7:23). They had no true relationship with the Lord, therefore, He did not know or recognize them. So, the days of the coming of Christ will be just as it was in the days of Noah; the entrance to the ark was shut by the hand of God, the righteous were saved, and the wicked were condemned and entered into divine judgment.

The foolish were professing believers that honored Christ with their lips, yet their hearts were far from Him, worshiping the Lord in vain with an empty profession and no substance to their testimony; virgins calling themselves Christian believers, yet they chose not to maintain close fellowship or walk with the Lord in their natural lives. They did not keep their inner lives under the control of the Holy Spirit; therefore, they were not ready to serve with Christ in His kingdom. The oil represents the Holy Spirit in the life of a believer, and none can share the Holy Spirit with one another, each must prepare and have their own supply for their personal walk with the Lord in order to follow Him and do His will in the earth.

Every believer will either be a wise virgin or a foolish virgin who were to prepare to meet the Lord and be rewarded with a grand entrance into the eternal kingdom of Christ (Matt. 25:1-13). The foolish virgins awoke to a great surprise and found out that, in truth, they were not ready or prepared to meet the Lord. In a final sentence from the Lord Himself, they were rejected and shut out of the kingdom age and cast into outer darkness, a place of sorrow, loss, and estrangement from Christ where there is no light, only unrelenting darkness, and hopelessness. Everything about your salvation and deliverance in this generation depends on your relationship with Christ.

Many have been called today but few have chosen to take heed to that heavenly call (Matt. 22:14). We that are alive today are an end-time people living in the time of the Lord's sudden return. We also have a great calling that requires a greater responsibility than all other generations. This generation of saints has been given much and much will be required from them for, as Jesus said, "To whom much is given much will also be required," and "that servant who knew his master's will, and did not prepare *himself* or do according to his will, shall be beaten with many *stripes*. But he who did not know, yet committed things deserving of stripes, shall be beaten with few. For everyone to whom much is given, from him much will be required; and to whom much has been committed, of him they will ask the more" (Luke 12:47-48 NKJV).

If believers do not truly love God and do not obey or keep His word in this generation, they will find themselves shut out of Christ's kingdom without the Lord's protection and left in great despair without Christ in the earth. They will be left in the hands of the enemies of God who will punish them, and they will be beaten with many lashes. If a believer will make Christ their Lord and walk with Him in a holy relationship in this life, you can be assured that they will live together with Him forever and, because they live holy before Him and all men now in this life, they will most assuredly be blessed and a partaker of the first resurrection (Rev. 20:5-6).

This book is a prophetic warning to those that are not walking uprightly before the Lord nor living according to His will. Those that have turned away from serving the Lord should consider their ways and turn back to Him quickly with repentance of heart so they can fulfill the commandment of Jesus to "love the Lord your God with all your heart and with all your soul and with all your mind. This is the first and greatest commandment" (Matt. 22:37-38 NIV). Jesus said, "If you love me, you will keep my commandments" (John 14:15), and "If anyone loves Me, he will keep My word; and My Father will love him, and We will come to him and make Our home with him. He who does not love Me does not keep My words; and the word which you hear is not Mine but the Father's who sent Me" (John 14:23-24 NKJV).

Scripture References
Chapter Fifteen

Acts 1:11 NASU Jesus Taken Up
Matt. 24:43 Watch For the Lord's Coming
Eph. 5:15-20 NIV Be Careful
Luke 12:35-40 ESV In An Hour You Do Not Expect
Matt. 7:23 I Know You Not
Matt. 25:1-13 The Parable of the Virgins
Matt. 22:14 Many Are Called
Luke 12:47-48 NKJV To Whom Much is Given
Rev. 20:5-6 The First Resurrection
Matt. 22:37-38 NIV The Greatest Commandment
John 14:15 Keep My Commandments
John 14:23-24 NKJV Keep My Word

The Battle For Your Souls

In this last and final generation, the saints who were born for this season have been chosen to face the kingdom of the antichrist. "But you have an anointing from the Holy One, and all of you know the truth. I do not write to you because you do not know the truth, but because you do know it and because no lie comes from the truth. Who is the liar? It is the man who denies that Jesus is the Christ. Such a man is the antichrist—he denies the Father and the Son. No one who denies the Son has the Father; whoever acknowledges the Son has the Father also" (1 John 2:20-22 NIV). The antichrist beast system will war against the end-time saints for forty-two months namely the Great Tribulation. The true saints of God have entered into a great war, not of their choosing, the war has come to us because we hold the testimony of Jesus, and the enemy knows very well that we are the Lord's army in the earth. "And the dragon was wroth with the woman, and went to make war with the remnant of her seed, which keep the commandments of God, and have the testimony of Jesus Christ" (Rev. 12:17 KJV).

Many today preach and believe a secret rapture will take place before we see any tribulation or trouble, yet many are seeing trouble and great trials now. Rest assured, our faith will soon be tried and tested. It is through our faith and patient endurance that we will inherit all that the Father has promised to us and not one hair on our head will perish. We must remember the words of Jesus saying, "As it was in the days of Noah, so it will be at the coming of the Son of Man. For in the days before the flood, people were eating and drinking, marrying, and giving in marriage, up to the day Noah entered the ark. They knew nothing about what would happen until the flood came and took them all away. That is how it will be at the coming of the Son of Man" (Matt. 24:37-39 NIV). Noah was not taken out of the world, he was protected during the great judgment and preserved through the flood. The same happened with Lot. God protected Abraham, his friend, as he watched God's fiery judgment fall upon the wicked. It was through Abraham's prayers that Lot was saved, yet because he was in the wrong place, he lost everything. No matter what one believes, we must let no man deceive us. We, God's people, must fully trust God and be ready to endure to the end knowing we will be delivered whether by life or by death. We must, in this world, not love our lives unto death and we will receive a crown of eternal life (Matt. 10:22; Rev. 3:11).

We are about to face the greatest struggle we have ever been in as we contend with the princes, the powers, and rulers of the darkness of this world and spiritual wickedness in high places (Eph. 6:12) while Satan, the prince and power of this world and prince and power of the air, seeks to take control of every mind on this planet. He will manipulate the nations with cunning, craftiness, deceit, and witchcraft with the objective being to discredit the Godhead and causing people to rebel against the heavenly order that God established. Satan's intent is to paralyze people with fear in order to seduce mankind to worship the antichrist and his system. "And they worshipped the dragon which gave power unto the beast: and they worshipped the beast, saying, Who is like unto the beast? who is able to make war with him? And there was given unto him a mouth speaking great things and blasphemies; and power was given unto him to continue forty and two months. And he opened his mouth in blasphemy against God, to blaspheme his name, and his tabernacle, and them that dwell in heaven. And it was given unto him to make war with the saints, and to overcome them: and power was given him over all kindreds, and tongues, and nations. And all that dwell upon the earth shall worship him, whose names are not written in the book of life of the Lamb slain from the foundation of the world. If any man has an ear, let him hear" (Rev. 13:4-9 KJV).

One of the greatest struggles we have is in our own minds. We are facing a daily diabolical and psychological assault against our minds, our wills, and our emotions. Fear and intimidation are the devil's greatest weapons. Everyday our minds and senses are attacked by bad news of numerous wars, conflicts and "the sky is falling" kind of mentality declaring all will be lost even though the Prince of Peace rules the heavens and the earth. "And the peace of God, which transcends all understanding, will guard your hearts and your minds in Christ Jesus" (Phil. 4:7 NIV). The devil is the father of lies and a liar from the beginning and, not only the devil, but the religious leaders of Jesus's day because they believed the lies, and enforced the devil's lies by attacking and slandering Jesus and His saints. That is why those that adhere to lies and falsehoods are called the children of the wicked one and liars like their father the devil (John 8:44; Matt. 13:38).

In this last hour the saints of God must be very courageous and with all diligence, we must be able to separate lies from the truth. God's Word is truth, and we are to meditate on it day and night which will give us the victory in life and in death (Josh. 1:8). "Finally, my brethren, be strong in the Lord, and in the power of his might. Put on the whole armor of God that ye may be able to stand against the wiles of the devil. For we wrestle not against flesh and blood, but against principalities, against powers, against the rulers of the darkness of this world, against spiritual wickedness in high places. Wherefore take unto you the whole armor of God that ye may be able to withstand in the evil day, and having done all, to stand. Stand therefore, having your loins girt about with truth, and having on the breastplate of righteousness" (Eph. 6:10-14 KJV).

Scripture References
Chapter Sixteen

1 John 2:20-22 NIV Who is a Liar?

Rev. 12:17 KJV The Dragon Makes War

Matt. 24:37-39 NIV As In the Days of Noah

Matt. 10:22 Hated For My Name

Rev. 3:11 Hold Fast

Eph. 6:12 Spiritual Wickedness in High Places

Rev. 13:4-9 The Dragon

Phil. 4:7 NIV The Peace of God

John 8:44 The Father of Lies

Matt. 13:38 The Good Seed

Josh. 1:8 Meditate on God's Law

Eph. 6:10-14 KJV The Whole Armor of God

Victory in the Time of Trouble

This is the generation that will enter and experience the Great Tribulation Jesus spoke about. It will be a time of trouble such has never been seen since the beginning of the world. "For then there will be great tribulation, such as has not been since the beginning of the world until this time, no, nor ever shall be" (Matt. 24:21 NKJV). The Great Tribulation is the last three-and-one-half years of time before Christ returns in power and great glory to judge the kings of the earth and to repay vengeance upon His enemies. "When the Lord Jesus will be revealed from heaven with His mighty angels in flaming fire, dealing out retribution to those who do not know God and to those who do not obey the gospel of our Lord Jesus. These will pay the penalty of eternal destruction, away from the presence of the Lord and from the glory of His power, when He comes to be glorified in His saints on that day, and to be marveled at among all who have believed for our testimony to you was believed" (2 Thess. 1:7b-11 NASU).

In the time we are living, the antichrist and his evil economic system are rising to forcibly rule over the whole earth. The Apostle John and Prophet Daniel give us significant understanding about this time, and it is when the ten kings that have received no kingdom, as of yet, receive power for one hour or forty-two months in biblical time. These ten kings have one mind and shall give their power and strength to the beast, the antichrist. These ten kings are now in the earth ready to give their power to the beast. The reason these kings have no kingdom is because they have not been elected by a sovereign country, these are men with great power and wealth that they use to buy nations and people causing them to sell out to the devil's evil plans of ruin and destruction. Through the empowerment of Satan, these kings that have sold themselves for evil will be given a platform to use witchcraft and sorcery to deceive, manipulate, and mislead all peoples and every nation on earth. These kings will make war with the Lamb, who is a man of war, and Jesus will come not this time as a lamb but as the roaring Lion of the tribe of Judah. He will overcome them: for He is Lord of lords and King of kings: and those that are with Him are called, chosen, and faithful to the end (Matt. 24:21; Rev. 17:12, 14).

This is the time the saints must endure and stand with our mouths filled with praise and a life of full obedience to the cause of Christ while we love not our own lives even unto death. "Because you have kept my word in quiet strength, I will keep you from the hour of testing, which is coming on the entire world, to put to the test those who are on earth. I come quickly: keep that which you have, so that no one may take your crown. Him who overcomes I will make a pillar in the house of my God, and he will go out no more: and I will put on him the name of my God, and the name of the town of my God, the new Jerusalem, which comes down out of heaven from my God, and my new name. He who has ears, let him give ear to what the Spirit says to the churches" (Rev. 3:10-14 BBE). Through faith and courage, we must do all to withstand the attacks and onslaughts of the enemy. We should choose our battles wisely for we know all are not friends to us or the Lord.

The Father has not promised to take us out of this world, but He has promised to keep us and protect the faithful in the hour of tribulation. It is during the time of the Great Tribulation, that is even now upon us, that the Lord will judge the world in righteousness and repay vengeance to His enemies (Ps. 98:9). "For the day of vengeance *is* in My heart, And the year of My redeemed has come" (Isa. 63:4 NKJV). This is a great time for those that believe and a place we can take heart and be encouraged for it is also the time of the Lord's redeemed, a time when all the things that are written will be fulfilled. "For these be the days of vengeance, that all things which are written may be fulfilled" (Luke 21:22 KJV). Jesus will come to be glorified in His saints and admired by all who have believed.

"Therefore, is the kingdom of heaven likened unto a certain king, which would take account of his servants" (Matt. 18:23 KJV). The day of accountability and reckoning for our deeds is upon us. As the Father gathers all things together, He will first call His leaders into account and then every believer will give an account according to the talents they received from the Master. Very soon the time will come that every leader and every church system will have to submit themselves to an appointed leadership chosen and ordained of God. Churches will no longer be islands unto themselves and no longer will they be accountable to themselves alone for the government of Christ will be complete and set up in earth as the Lord has promised.

It is those that keep Christ's commandments that can hear His voice when He speaks or warns us, and this will be important when the need arises to escape trouble or danger. "Because you have kept my command to persevere, I also will keep you from the hour of trial which shall come upon the whole world, to test those who dwell on the earth. Behold, I am coming quickly! Hold fast what you have, that no one may take your crown" (Rev. 3:10-11 NKJV). Those that yield to the Holy Spirit are filled with the spirit of truth and will not be deceived or led into error, "for as many as are led by the Spirit of God, they are the sons of God" and overcomers in this life (Rom. 8:14 KJV). If the believer in Christ keeps the Word of God and holds tightly to His commandments, they will be more than conquerors in this life and shall never see death. God will always cause them to triumph and win the victory in Christ Jesus (2 Cor. 2:14).

Scripture References
Chapter Seventeen

Matt. 24:21 NKJV Great Tribulation

2 Thess. 1:7b-11 NASU When Jesus is Revealed

Matt. 24:21 Great Tribulation

Rev. 17:12, 14 War With the Lamb

Rev. 3:10-14 BBE He Who Has an Ear

Ps. 98:9 He Will Judge

Isa. 63:4 NKJV Day of Vengeance

Luke 21:22 KJV Days of Vengeance

Matt. 18:23 KJV Accountability

Rev. 3:10-122 NKJV Hold Fast

Rom 8:14 KJV Sons of God

2 Cor. 2:14 Thanks Be to God

AACML

The Apostolic Association of Churches, Ministers and Leaders International

The Apostolic Association of Churches, Ministers and Leaders International (AACML) was created by the Lord over thirty years ago. Chief Apostles Dr.'s John and Kim Neuhaus through AACML and Neuhaus Ministries International (NMI) provide apostolic covenant covering to Apostles, Bishops, Prophets, five-fold ministry leaders, CEO'S, and business leaders globally. AACML provides training, development, and ministry planting globally.

AACML is a body of believers and followers of the Lord Jesus Christ. The message of AACML is the message of the gospel of the Lord Jesus Christ, and His kingdom government. AACML empowers leaders globally. It ordains, activates, appoints, and authenticates legitimate ministry and business.

AACML has active ministry throughout the United States of America, and is actively proficient in over fourteen nations globally, as we harvest the nations for the kingdom of God. We are thankful for the fruitfulness and growth that continues to thrive in AACML. Hundreds of ministries have been planted and many businesses have been launched. Over the years, we have established and supported our own orphanages, directed major global humanitarian efforts, planted Bible Colleges (internationally) and Schools of the Apostles and Prophets, and hosted international crusades and evangelism meetings.

We currently successfully develop and strengthen over 2,000 ministries and businesses and their powerful leadership. We train leaders in kingdom servanthood and excellence. We are committed to global evangelism, supporting works throughout the world—planting churches, raising up new leadership, and empowering new entrepreneurs.

Chief Apostles Dr.'s John and Kim Neuhaus have been called by God for this unique and empowering ministry. They committedly serve their sons and daughters in the faith. AACML is an end-time apostolic and prophetic ministry of love as God is love.

Jesus is LORD.

Contact Information

We look forward to hearing from you. For more information, contact us at:

- Aacml.com
- aacmlglobal@gmail.com
- 561-427-5530

❖ **AACML Monthly International Leaders Meeting**

Chief Apostle Dr. John Neuhaus and AACML hosts a monthly international ZOOM meeting, for a time of revelation and impartation, where many leaders gather together in the spirit of unity. You are invited to join us. Email us, call or text us at the above contact information.

❖ **Zion International Bible College**

Master Classes, School of the Apostles
Master Classes, School of the Prophets
Five Fold Ministry Leadership and Development
For enrollment information, Email us, call or text us at the above contact information.

❖ **AACML Annual International Apostolic & Prophetic Summit**

AACML's annual global gathering of leaders is held in July in South Florida in the USA. For registration information, Email us, call or text us at the above contact information.

Don't miss out!

Visit the website below and you can sign up to receive emails whenever john neuhaus publishes a new book. There's no charge and no obligation.

https://books2read.com/r/B-A-PLHY-YUYIC

BOOKS 2 READ

Connecting independent readers to independent writers.

9 798890 344212